# COLLEGE WITHOUT STUDENT LOANS

"We were very pleased with everything Dave helped us accomplish for our Daughter. She started out not knowing what direction she wanted to pursue… and with the use of the MCP Program and the CAP Program, she found her passion, and direction, and is attending a college that we thought we never would be able to afford. Dave was brilliant with the strategies he suggested to increase our Financial Aid. All told… we saved waaaaay beyond the $50,000 they guarantee. We are honored to give our recommendation."

**—Mandy and Dale W.**

"I had met with 2 other so-called "college Planning" companies… in fact; one of those companies was referred to us from the High School my son attended. We retained the services of one of the companies… but never got any benefit from their services or from the financial end of things. I attended the "Free Workshop," met with Dave for our "Free Private Consultation," and after listening to him present the services that College Funding Connection offered, and the results they were getting, I decided to give them a shot.

I figured I had nothing to lose… after all they offered a "Written Guarantee." What began sounding like something "too good to be true" ended up being one of the most remarkable decisions I've ever made in my life. Not only did they deliver on what they promised… they over-delivered, and hit a grand-slam home run with my younger son. In fact… the strategies they implemented even lowered the cost of college for my older son—who was already attending a 4-year college up north. I'd do it all over again… but I would have used College Funding Connection the first time around."

**—Theresa and Stephen J**

"I can only tell you—I am absolutely amazed at what Dave was able to accomplish with our son, and our situation! Now…I will admit, I am very proud of what my son was also able to accomplish… but we would have never known about the colleges, and which were the best "Fit" for our son, nor would we have ever gotten the Financial Aid we are now getting. Dave doesn't beat around the bush when it comes to direction and what needs to take place. Everything they do is outlined, planned, and implemented ahead of schedule. My best advice to any parent would be to simply let go, and let these guys do their magic. You won't be disappointed! This is a service that has been needed by parents for quite some time, and there is no one better in the country than Dave… and College Funding Connection! "

**—Brent and Melissa M**

"It is truly an honor to be included in the Testimonials pages of College Funding Connection website. Honestly… I don't know where to begin. From the start—everything and I mean everything was discussed. Dave asked some really tough questions to our son. These were the types of questions that most definitely need to be addressed before your child ever leaves the house. We had fun through the entire process yet Dave was very serious about how to get things done.

That probably sums everything up. College Funding Connection knows what they are doing, and they do it better than anyone else I have found. We felt totally comfortable throughout the process, both my wife and I slept a lot better once we decided to go forward with College Funding Connection. They did an amazing job! "

**—Christopher Michael W**

"Well our story is a bit different—we have twins and needless to say, both my husband and I were more than a little nervous about college. Figuring out how to afford to be able to pay for college for one child is hard enough but when you have two, well that kicks up the sleepless nights, and apprehensiveness to a completely new level! We attended a workshop, and took advantage of the private consultation, and the next thing you know it's like we were living again. No more stress, no more worries, and the further we went into the College Funding Connection program the better it got.

As it ended up our twins are attending the same very prestigious private college, and because of Dave's efforts we are paying only a fraction of what it would have cost us. I know for a fact we would have been paying at least twice as much as we are paying right now had we decided to attend a State college. So when you hear Dave say that you can attend a Private school for less than the cost of a State college it's all true. We were so happy with College Funding Connection that we have referred them to our friends and work associates with full confidence."

**—Kathy and Craig G**

"Here is what Nathan has gotten so far (These are only the initial acceptance letters):

- Baylor-$14K/yr. $56K/total-waiting to hear for Faculty Scholarship-full tuition
- St. Louis University-$16K/yr. $64K total-waiting to hear if he got the full tuition scholarship and early medical school acceptance
- TCU-yes, scholarship offers sent out in March
- Trinity University-$18K/yr. $72K total-plus opportunity to compete for full tuition scholarship
- Willamette-$22K/yr. $88K total-plus opportunity for service 75% tuition scholarship
- Austin College-$24K/yr. $98K total
- Waiting on Santa Clara, Centre College, and Cal Poly-SLO

Happy! And thank you!"

**—Randy and Gale C**

Testimonials such as these just keep pouring in. Put the secrets of *College Without Student Loans* to work for you. We'll be waiting to add your testimonial to our list.

You are about to learn just how much financial leverage you already have at hand in order to get into a college of your preference. It's just a matter of knowing the ropes, getting the right coaching, and applying the techniques that are revealed in the following pages.

# COLLEGE

## WITHOUT

# STUDENT
# LØANS

*Attend Your Ideal College & Make It
Affordable Regardless of Your Income*

# DAVE SMITH

NEW YORK

# COLLEGE WITHOUT STUDENT LOANS

*Attend Your Ideal College & Make It Affordable Regardless of Your Income*

ISBN 978-1-61448-633-6 paperback
ISBN 978-1-61448-634-3 eBook
Library of Congress Control Number: 2013931883

Morgan James Publishing
The Entrepreneurial Publisher
5 Penn Plaza, 23rd Floor
New York City, New York 10001
(212) 655-5470 office • (516) 908-4496 fax
www.MorganJamesPublishing.com

**Cover Design by:**
Rachel Lopez
www.r2cdesign.com

**Interior Design by:**
Bonnie Bushman
bonnie@caboodlegraphics.com

In an effort to support local communities, raise awareness and funds, Morgan James Publishing donates a percentage of all book sales for the life of each book to Habitat for Humanity Peninsula and Greater Williamsburg.

Get involved today, visit
www.MorganJamesBuilds.com.

# DEDICATION

To my wife Denise, whose support and suggestions were critical to the completion of this book.

Thank you Erica and Brandon for being my inspiration and hope.

And to mom for your challenge which continues to drive me.

For additional information and insights go to www.collegewithoutstudentloans.com

# CONTENTS

# FOREWORD
## *By Loral Langemeier*

WHERE WE'RE HEADED AS a nation is scary. Student loan debt is out of control and by some estimations is the next 'bubble.'

I went to college and got a Masters. I don't use it today.

I'm not a fan of college. Especially, if your sole purpose is to get a job. However, with that said, college is a great place to network, be surrounded by new ideas and find a career path in life that appeals to you.

Now, I'm not naïve enough to think that everyone should be an entrepreneur or would even want to. There are two kinds of people in the world and we need both–Entrepreneurs and Employees. We entrepreneurs need employees and good ones at that. This book will help create good employees.

This book is for parents who want their children to go to college. It would be negligent on my part not to recommend it to you as a way to save money. The number one problem graduates face isn't finding a job...It's paying back their student loans BECAUSE they haven't been able to find a job in their chosen vocation.

They end up taking 'whatever' job comes their way to pay their bills—namely student loans. Think. If your child were able to go to college and graduate without a single student loan, how would this affect their employment possibilities? They wouldn't need to settle for the first job that came their way. They wouldn't get stuck in the 'I-have-a-job-and-am-paying-back-my-student-loans-right-now-so-I-can't-look-for-a-better-one' trap.

I hope you're starting to see the power that lies within these pages. The power to financially free your children.

Take lots of notes!

— **Loral Langemeier**
5 Time – New York Times Best Selling Author

# ACKNOWLEDGEMENTS

THE MOST WONDERFUL ASPECT of this journey is the people I have had the good fortune to learn from and work with each day. I am incredibly blessed to be able to interface and network with tremendously talented professionals daily. Every person who has ever written a book understands it is a daunting task which requires a team effort to accomplish. The bottom line is that I want to thank everyone who helped me research, write, and publish this book.

This includes and is not limited to Susan Sparks for your structure and getting me started. My friend Harushi Tetsuka, one of the most creative people in my life for getting me to the finish line. Les Thomas for your input, ideas, and effort in our creation of a one-of-a-kind process that has helped so many families. Brad Wood for teaching me the best ways to implement technology, Aloha my friend.

The most fantastic participant in this journey is my wife Denise who through bad times and good times has always stood by me and supported my efforts. Not only are you my life partner, you add strength to my resolve and purpose to succeed by helping others prosper everyday (HOPE).

# INTRODUCTION

IT STARTS ON THE Little League diamond, on the gridiron, in the gymnasium, or on the athletic field: the dream of college scouts, a free ride education, and a highly paid career as a professional athlete. Hours devoted to practice and traveling to games come at the expense of family life, academics, and other activities, all for the chance at the golden ticket.

My goal and sole focus was to play professional baseball. My dream was to be drafted by Major League Baseball right out of high school and college became a secondary, if not a distant thought. Everything was working out as planned; I was a top starting pitcher and player on multi-championship teams, All-Star and All League selections.

Then the unthinkable happened. Two weeks prior to the MLB Amateur Draft in 1974 I became injured, tearing the rotator cuff in my pitching shoulder. At that time there were no known surgical procedures to repair the damage, thus my dreams of a Major League career…crushed.

Time to Implement Plan B.

I had several athletic scholarship offers from various colleges to play football at certain schools and baseball at other schools and even some wanting me to play both sports. I had plenty of offers but in the end it didn't matter. I wrote letters to all the schools that offered scholarships and respectfully declined their offers.

## MY STORY

My parents met while attending Ventura City College got married and then decided that my mother would give up her career ambitions and go to work so my father could graduate with a Metallurgical Engineering degree. Each had their own differing ideas for my college education which was news to me. My mother wanted me to live at home and attend the local state university while they paid for my education. (Keep in mind that this was the 70's and college was less expensive then.) My father was the first in his family to earn a college degree and his attitude was; "I worked and paid for my education so too will my sons." Mom and Dad were not on the same page for my college education which created a huge conflict in our home. Unfortunately this only came to light when it was time to have already made decisions regarding college.

Time to Implement Plan C.

Plan C consisted of me moving out of my parent's home and pursuing both baseball and an education. I spent a year rehabbing my arm in an attempt to come back from injury while attending a private university as a freshman. Unfortunately my efforts to play again were in vain as I was unable to recover my previous competitive level.

Private school was $30,000 a year which was something I could not afford. I transferred to a state college my sophomore year and worked full time while foregoing collegiate athletics.

Since I realized athletics would not be my golden ticket I focused on academics and earned a scholarship to study abroad during my junior year at the University of Upsala in Sweden. The experience of living and studying abroad was absolutely the best learning decision I had made in my life. After attending two academic years in Europe I returned for my senior year at the local state university in southern California and graduated with a Bachelor of Science degree in Business Management.

Looking back on this time of my life I realize that my greatest accomplishment was that I completed a tremendous curriculum without incurring any student loans.

## HOW?

I worked my way through college creatively seeking opportunities that allowed me to adapt my schedule so that I could work the graveyard shift, attend morning classes, and catch up on sleep in the afternoon.

While it took me five years to complete my college education as some of the study abroad credits didn't transfer, I think it's safe to say that completing a degree without any debt is an accomplishment whether it's finished in four years or forty.

Fast forward 30 years and the college outlook for most high school students seems dismal at best. Many parents are still paying off their own college loan debt and have no clue how to help their children afford college. Competition for elite athletic scholarships is fierce and the prospect of a pro athlete career has about the same odds as winning the lottery. Most students and parents assume that student loans are the only way to finance an education so it's not surprising that student loan debt now surpasses credit card debt. Current college graduates are so far in debt that they will not be able to afford home ownership and the prospect of living debt free is unthinkable.

Parents and students are asking the same question- How does one get a college degree without going broke?

Parents and students are asking the same question – How does one get a college degree without going broke? Fortunately, it's not as unattainable as it may seem. This book is here to say yes–There is Hope!

In fact elite, private universities are begging to pay the way for students. Believe it or not students can be in the driver's seat when it comes to selecting a school and financing their college education.

In my private consulting practice I've seen countless families realize their dreams of a college education come true and I will share the strategies and steps I use to help them achieve those goals. I will outline the S-A-F-E process that I use with my clients and share the secrets that state colleges don't want you to know.

I will challenge your mindset on sending your student to the typical state or local college by inviting you to explore the opportunities that a "pricier" college holds. More importantly you'll discover that these desirable colleges will actually make an education very easy and affordable if you know what they are looking for and how your son or daughter fits those criteria.

I will also challenge you as a parent to consider that your plans for your student's college education may be vastly different from theirs. I encourage you to begin the conversation early – not after the last of the high school graduation party favors are packed away.

Whether a client is sitting in my office discussing college funding plans or they're reading this book my intention is the same – to help students and their parents discover opportunities and colleges that are outside the typical path of state school and staggering student loan debt.

In the following pages you will see how important a good fit is to ensuring a student finds a school that meets not only their academic needs but their social, cultural, and financial needs as well. You will gain an understanding of the school's position on admissions in concert with their bottom line. You will learn how the unique qualities of your student get the school's attention in addition to their grades and test scores.

We often hear the phrase; "It's never too early to start planning for college." It's true but doing it properly involves more than just opening a savings account. Implementing the strategies for positioning your student as desirable to colleges is a vital part of this process and starting them as early-on as possible is a key element.

Chapter One

# It's Arithmetic

Former president Bill Clinton entertained the American people with one of the most enthusiastic speeches of his life during the 2012 Democratic Convention. Political beliefs aside this is a speech I will remember for quite some time because I was captivated by the clear, concise, and understandable message. He had so much fun with just two words, "It's Arithmetic".

My goal is to have a meaningful impact on you with the same two words. When talking about funding a college education today "It's Arithmetic" or in this book I'll call it "Dave's Math." And here are key facts to keep in mind:

Average Cost of Attendance (COA) $40,000+
Average Time to Graduate (Undergrad Degree) 5.8 years

Average Cost for Undergrad Degree $232,000
Average Student Loan Debt-Approximately $30,000+

By now you know that there is no manual on how to be a parent and even if there were a chapter on getting your kids out of the door and off to college it would be vastly different from your parent's experience with your college education. Times have changed.

In your drive and determination to be a good parent you most likely enrolled your children in piano lessons, paid for orthodontics, and bought various trinkets from the school fundraisers. As your child gets ready to leave the nest you, like many parents, may feel like throwing your hands in the air and let whatever happens happen in the college enrollment process.

College is vastly different from your own experience 30, or even 20 years ago. The process, the expense, and the competition are different today. Back in the day you took the ACT or SAT and filled out a few applications, then either worked part time to help pay for college or signed your life away with student loans.

Today there is the need to oversee timelines, application deadlines, fees, FAFSA filings, and CSS reports while motivating your teenager who only hears "blah, blah, blah" above the drone of peer pressure, hormones, and video games.

As parents have come to realize the sheer amount of time, research, and funds the college application process entails, many are turning to outside services to guide them through the process.

It is something I highly recommend not just as one who is in this line of work but because those families that I've assisted have all emphatically had the same reaction—"We'd be stupid to do this on our own."

Let me provide a few cautionary guidelines before you start your search:

The industry is still fairly new so there are no governing bodies that certify college placement entities. With so many facets involved in the process most professionals focus on one segment such as essay coaching, taking SAT/ACTs, or financial aid rather than cover the full gamut of requirements.

Choose your planner just as you would choose any other professional service such as your tax preparer, doctor, or lawyer. A former teacher or counselor's training and background is better suited to work with students through the test preparation and essay process. Conversely a C.P.A. or business person who has no teaching or counseling training would be more adept at assisting parents through the financial process.

Keeping the intent of attending an elite school in mind you should consult multiple persons to accomplish admission and financial aid requirements. Assembling a dream team of professionals to make it happen is not only possible but is well worth the investment. My organization partners with local and national subject matter experts including college counselors, admissions personnel, and essay and testing experts. In essence I manage college prep dream teams.

In order to fully understand the team participation and dynamics of this process we'll use the bicycle as a metaphor. Picture a bicycle-the student represent the front wheel because they control the direction and the parents represent the back wheel because they provide the power. You need both parts to get anywhere.

*I met with the Clark family early in their son John's high school career. While they were confident that their son had the potential to get into an elite college they also realized that there was a lot that they didn't know even though Dad was a professional financial planner. Working through our network John and his parents received coaching, support, and financial education that would ultimately result in a hefty merit-based financial aid package. Through the process his parents realized that positioning their son on their own would have been like taking on another full-time job.*

*Their investment paid off: John was accepted to an Ivy League school with a 95% cost of attendance valued at over $250,000 for four years. The family's investment was a mere $8,000! Would you invest $8,000 to get that kind of return? Can you put a value on a Harvard, MIT, or Duke education and understand the difference it can make over a person's lifetime?*

*If you're still not convinced ask yourself where else could I invest $8,000 and receive a 312% rate of return?*

Students currently entering state universities rely heavily on financial aid. Many schools expect that 70-80% of their students will access financial aid. Most parents have no clue where to start in terms of accessing needs-based and merit-based awards. Looking to their high schools for answers won't help much. I'll make a very bold statement that unfortunately is true: high schools don't understand how to get financial aid-as a parent you are wise to seek out those who do understand the process.

Just as consulting a professional tax strategist as opposed to using a do-it-yourself software program can potentially minimize your tax liabilities, engaging a qualified college planner will save you tens of thousands of dollars and dramatically increase the odds that your student will complete their degree in a traditional four-year plan.

There are many pitfalls surrounding the college admissions process. Understanding scholarships and academic awards is one of the most puzzling and frustrating of those for parents.

Here's an example of what happened to Lynn, a bright and gifted student who had been active in her community.

*Lynn had been accepted to a state university complete with an academic award of $15,000. As her high school graduation approached she received a $1,500 scholarship from the local Rotary Club. Lynn and her parents were banking on the fact that she now had $16,500 to apply to her tuition and fees that fall. The University*

*then deducted the $1,500 from her academic award and Lynn was back to $15,000.*

*Frustrating? Yes. Fair? Yes, in the eyes of the university. Their academic award was the school's way of discounting their costs for the student. When she was able to contribute an additional $1,500 the school reasoned that their discount didn't need to be so deep.*

The planner and their team serve as a coach to help your student maneuver the intricate path to matriculation. The information encompasses where to apply, specific areas of study, how to complete the applications, effective essay writing, and a clear picture of the admissions process along with what to expect all the way to the final stage which could be an interview at their dream school.

The sheer number of students following the herd mentality of attending state and local colleges reduces the amount of merit based and academic awards available there. Elite, selective, and competitive colleges typically perceived as too expensive or exclusive have ample means of discounting their tuition for those students deemed as desirable. Merit-based aid has no income requirement or limitations; it's the school's subjective decision. The more valuable your student is to them the more they will discount their services in order to secure their attendance.

Up to this point schooling your children was relatively easy. Most likely all you had to do was to register them at the local public school and make sure they showed up for the first day of class. While that statement is over-simplistic the college process is a whole new challenge. While the work of keeping up with what needs to be completed, submitted, and executed is daunting and time consuming, too many families leave this one life-process up to chance.

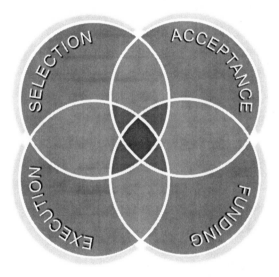

## The S-A-F-E Way

Selection, Acceptance, Funding and Execution, or S-A-F-E will give you a better understanding of what's involved and how a professional planner can assist you. Regardless of whether you are prepared financially or emotionally to send your child off to college, the day the high school says "You're done, don't come

⌐re before you know it. The good news is that ⌐ill time to position your student for success.

## Elite? Selective? Competitive?

There are approximately 2,000 non-profit institutions in the U.S. College and university system. There is a specific breakdown of how schools are ranked. Schools such as Stanford, Harvard, MIT, Duke, Vanderbilt, Yale and Pomona are some of the 50 "Elite" schools. Next are 'Selective' schools made up of roughly 150 colleges including USC, Cal, UCLA, Santa Clara, Cal Tech, and Pitzer. The third category is made up of approximately 250 'Competitive' colleges such as Pepperdine, USD, Occidental, LMU and UC Davis. The remaining 1,750 are basic, standard colleges, such as state schools and universities. The purpose of this book is to help you align your student's unique talents and abilities with an elite, selective, or competitive school that will offer attractive admissions and financial aid packages.

For more information regarding the S-A-F-E Way go to:
www.collegewithoutstudentloans.com/safe.html

Chapter 2

# SELECTION

Ray was 'Mr. Everything' on the football field in high school. He was MVP during his senior year when his high school team won the sectional championship. Recruiters from around the western states courted Ray with the intention of getting him to attend their school and play football.

Besides his ability to play football Ray was a moderately good student with a 3.1 GPA and a 1570 SAT score. As a result he had so many options for college from various schools that he was overwhelmed and not sure how to proceed.

Not sure who to consult Ray sought guidance from his high school coach who urged him to accept a scholarship to attend college in Montana. Ray's coach had a good friend on the coaching staff in

*Montana and believed playing for a perennial championship team would offer professional opportunities to Ray in the future.*

*Ray's parents preferred he stay close to home and the relatives that supported the family. They had moved to the United States from Samoa when Ray was two years old and had never even travelled outside of southern California. They didn't clearly understand the difference in schools or what moving to a new location entailed.*

*Based upon his coach's recommendation however, Ray accepted the scholarship to attend the University of Montana.*

*By April of the next year one of Ray's former high school football coaches saw him working as a box boy at a local grocery store. The coach asked Ray, "Why aren't you in Montana?"*

*Ray's response was, "I missed my family and came home for good." Living in Montana was a culture shock for Ray without any family support. Most of the years he was growing up Ray would wear tank tops, gym shorts, and tennis shoes. In Montana the climate required layers of clothing Ray was not prepared for and couldn't afford. Being alone for the first time in his life he became depressed and eventually flunked out of school.*

**No other decision has such lasting academic and financial impact as the choice of the college your student attends.** Most families use emotional criteria such as a school's proximity to home, school reputation, or even the best football team in order to pick a college and just assume that the student will fit right in. (Remember my mother's idea that I'd live at home and go to community college?) They are not aware that there are schools out there that will be a good fit due to class size, major offerings, environment, and overall attitude.

In Ray's case his moving far away coupled with a drastic climate and cultural change proved too much of an adjustment. Yet for other students this type of stretch could result in a very positive outcome.

If you want your son or daughter to finish college in four years rather than become a professional student by dragging out the degree pursuit for seven or more years then sit up and pay close attention.

The intent of your child acquiring an education by getting a college degree is goal one and needs to be kept in mind. Parental influence can confuse a student's decision-making process. You may think you are encouraging your fledgling to get a good college education but the subtle undertones of your pep talk may send mixed messages: "go to college; just don't get too far from home."

Peers, older siblings, and conventional wisdom often don't do incoming freshman any favors. In Ray's situation his coach's advice didn't take into account Ray's strong family dynamic and the loss of his support system if he moved out of state. Another student however, may have thrived in the new climate far from home. People are different.

Start this conversation early and help your student weigh the pros and cons of staying close to home or attending school across the country. It's a discussion that will benefit both you and your student in the early process of selecting a school.

Consider a school's reputation as being difficult, a party school, or other stereotype at this time. Assuming that elite private schools are expensive and therefore not an option is a mistake in the selection process.

As I previously mentioned many elite private schools are more than willing to provide financial aid based on a student's fit. As you will see in the financial chapter many "expensive" schools have more Free Money available than the perceived bargain-priced state schools.

**Nearly 54% of college freshman will not return for their junior year primarily due to unhappiness with their college choice or because of financial pressures.**

Documented daily in newspapers across the county is the fact that American students are falling prey to the "herd mentality" by attending local colleges. The feeling that there is safety in numbers works against them as they sit in a class of 350 people in a dimly lit lecture hall and nod off while sitting in the back row.

## Is that the investment you had in mind?

Recently William G. Tierney wrote in the CHRONICLE of Higher Education; "Distance learning begins after the 5th row." Large universities scrambling to meet expenses are cramming more and more students into lecture setting where students never have any direct interaction with the professor.

"The opportunities to learn from other students and professors, in and out of class, are declining at the very time that we know such engagement is critical for learning. Shrinking state budgets have intensified this development, as boards, administrators,, and faculty, have largely agreed that one logical response is to increase class size."

Care must be taken when considering Cost versus Price. (Please refer to diagram above) School A graduates average 4.3 years of attendance and School B graduates average 5.9 years of attendance. Even though the cost of attendance (COA) of School A is an additional $6,000 it is the more cost effective institution when an additional 1.6 years of attendance at the less expensive school is eliminated.

In addition to class size as a selection factor one must consider the atmosphere or personality of the college as well. Yale or MIT will have a different level of intellect than the University of Illinois. Students may be intimidated about joining a more highly intelligent environment that forces them to constantly strain to keep up with the pack.

Pushing a student into a school that isn't in line with their maturity, capability, or intellect will frustrate them and can contribute to the dropout rate. This doesn't mean your student should settle into an academic environment that doesn't challenge them. Just as an overly challenging environment causes a student to lose interest they can become bored and lose interest when it's too easy.

A good balance of academic challenge, social interaction, and other intangibles will help a student grow. If the student is overwhelmed the right institution will provide additional resources to keep them going. The school will want to protect their investment. If a student gets into trouble academically they are moved to smaller study groups and receive tutoring and additional access to professors for more hands-on help rather than being moved to a larger class. A smaller class size facilitates learning for most people.

Is college right for every student? There is no one correct answer. Recent studies suggest that a college education will most often provide a higher income level, varied and increased career opportunities, and a higher level of personal satisfaction. So for most it's a way to help achieve their dreams and goals.

Setting expectations for your student to explore their career options is another conversation you should be having sooner rather than later. Having this conversation when they are in middle school isn't out of the question. Consider it time well invested that can pay dividends when a college presents an attractive offer to your student during their senior year of high school.

My dream of a professional athletic career 30 years ago is no different than the countless high school football, basketball, and baseball stars who are gambling on the chance that they will receive rock star status and the corresponding compensation that makes a college education an afterthought. While some do achieve that dream the majority realize through injury, like me, or culling, that there are only a limited number of golden tickets available through athletics.

Even if you cannot fathom the idea of your little one leaving the nest you aren't doing them any favors by saying things like; "How can anyone your age know what they want to do for the rest of their life?" Instead equip them with a skill set to ask questions, explore their options, and to make connections between their current interests and skills to those that translate into a career.

The aimless student who has no clear idea of a major or career path is at risk of becoming a seven-year student. Many parents hope their student will "find themselves" while away at college but often it's at great financial expense.

If your student hasn't answered the "Why College is Important for Them" question, or discovered their passion or career direction then it may not be in their best interest to go to college until they have a clear end goal. While that may sound harsh please consider that colleges, especially the elite institutions will not be inviting your student to attend at the college's expense. It doesn't mean that college won't ever be in the cards; it's just that your student may need to reassess, define some goals, and put a new plan into action.

For others, education doesn't always take place in a traditional university setting. Many students thrive in trade schools, entrepreneurial endeavors, apprenticeships, and military training.

It's safe to say many high school graduates don't "feel" ready to attend college because they were never encouraged to plan for it. Help them narrow it down. Exposure and experience help a student learn their individual comfort zones, interests, and passions. Parents can begin setting the expectation for college early in their child's grade school years. Ideally teachers, coaches, and peers reinforce that expectation continually through enhanced education. This "full court press" approach provides the highest probability of excellent results.

### How important is Passion? How does your student discover it and fashion that into a career?

Matching their career with what excites them is priceless. Many parents would argue that a young child couldn't possibly know what they should do later in life. Science asserts that children are always learning beginning at birth. Who says that it is too early to discover one's passion?

As early as in the 7th grade students can begin using tools that offer exposure and experience to help them discover careers that excite them. There are myriad resources available on the Internet and through school counselors to help students choose possible fields of study.

Hands-on real world experiences of shadowing a worker, volunteering, or work-study programs available while still in high school can often reveal likes and dislikes more quickly than any aptitude test. All of these can help shed light on a fulfilling career path and can boost your student's desirability to individual colleges depending on the activity.

## Is it the High School's job?

If you think that it's up to the high school to get your student ready for college and a career you'll probably be disappointed. **In California the ratio of students to high school counselors is on average in excess of 800:1**. It doesn't leave them much time to encourage your student to focus on college especially when the counselor's priority is to get your student graduated from high school and not necessarily being accepted into college.

The marketing done by colleges to high school students is not the most effective way to help your student make a wise selection either. The annual College Night Program is more like a trade show with free pens, colorful brochures, and lots of overwhelm and confusion for parents and students alike. Often the follow-up by those schools is ineffective mass marketing versus personal interviews and individual campus visits.

Brochures will flood your mailbox adding to the overwhelm students may feel when trying to make a decision. It's an inexpensive method that colleges use to market themselves and they are usually selling the lifestyle, the sports programs, and the environment but not necessarily communicating how they will equip your student with real world skills that will translate into a sustaining career.

# ARTS
# ACADEMICS
# ATHLETICS
# Activities

If your student excels in one of the Four As; Arts, Academics, Athletics, or Activities they'll receive even more marketing attention since those skills satisfy the institution's need. It's not a bad thing it's just important to know how those translate into improving your student's chances of being accepted at a school that is a good fit for them.

*Steve and Sharon have two boys; Scott, the oldest by two years, is very creative and Sam is the athlete in the family. Steve was adamant*

*about not sending any information to the federal government when it came time to submit the FAFSA form. His reasoning was that his privately owned business was successful financially and that it was a waste of time to apply for financial aid. This advice came from Steve's company tax advisor (CPA), who I found out later did not get financial aid for his own child so he assumed that Steve would not qualify for any aid as well.*

*Steve voiced his concerns regarding the FAFSA and stated his ability to pay whatever amount necessary in order for Scott to attend any school that he wanted to attend during a January meeting I had with the family. Steve simply felt that he made too much money in order for Scott to receive any aid and that it was a waste of time and energy to fill out the FAFSA. Sharon felt very differently and believed that any money saved off the cost of college could be utilized for graduate school or funding the next step in the boy's lives.*

*Selection of the schools that fit Scott well were specific in location, size of classes, ratio of students to professors, and time to graduation. These schools had to have at least a 50% probability of acceptance in order for Scott to make application. Based on this careful selection process I realized that "Need" based financial aid was not available for Scott but that "Merit" based financial aid would be possible even with a his 3.2 grade point average and a 1690 SAT score.*

*After reviewing all of Scott's personal achievements with Steve and Sharon it became clear that their son was well positioned at the selected schools to bring extreme value as an incoming freshman.*

*Scott was very active inside and outside of high school demonstrating leadership, problem solving, and qualities that indicated the uncommon maturity that this young man possessed.*

*After realizing Scott would not be eligible at some of the schools for merit aid if the FAFSA was not submitted, Steve then agreed to submit the FAFSA. The results were predictable as Scott received seven acceptances out of the eight schools he made applications to. Merit aid was offered in five of the schools' Student Aid Reports (SAR) at an average of $19,500 per year.*

*The decision to submit the FAFSA form in spite of their current income saved this family approximately $100,000.*

Time for some startling statistics:

- Less than 10% of freshmen entering college have a career direction.
- A study of college graduates indicates that 78% wished that they had majored in something other than the degree they earned.

As previously stated it's never too early to start the college selection process. If your student is a high school junior or senior you are behind the curve and need to start the planning process as quickly as possible. A lack of planning can lead to them having to accept a less than optimal offer from a local college or university that is not in yours or your student's best interest.

Without a clear career direction your student is at a greater disadvantage since a far greater number of schools require incoming freshmen to declare their major at the time of admission. It is expensive for a school to have a student change their major and the growing trend is that many schools do not allow or make it difficult and expensive for students to change their major along the path of earning a bachelor degree.

Selecting a career direction, a cluster of careers, or a major area of study is critical in choosing which school to attend. Not doing this increases the odds that your student defaults to the seven-year plan which not only increases the cost of their education but delays their entry into their future life.

## What if your son or daughter cannot decide?

What can your student do if they are undecided about a major? By examining their volunteer experiences, their club involvement, activities, and the hobbies that sparked their interest can help them discover their passions and talents. Finding their passion and developing their "Why" will make sure that the school they choose is a good fit before attending their first class in college.

Using their time in high school to develop interests and to make connections to a possible career path is one of the most effective ways for your student to fine-tune their decision process. Rather than arbitrarily deciding to become a doctor or lawyer this process helps them gain a better perspective of what they are truly interested in. It allows them to gain an understanding of what their career path entails and the options that are available within it.

Selecting the right school is a critical step in your student's education process so you really need to do your homework first. Let's review what needs to happen before your student begins to fill out application forms:

- Set the expectation-In families where college is an expectation from an early age, students rise to the challenge and select colleges, majors, and careers usually finishing college in four years.
- Fit, Fit, Fit-An education that fits your student's goals, aspirations, talents, and personality is priceless. This leads to happiness, contentment, higher productivity, and eventually to just the right career. Keep your eyes open for the clues.
- "Why" is more important than "How"-Your student needs to answer; Why am I going to college, why should I put forth the effort, why is it important? This helps provide the motivation necessary for a successful college experience.
- Utilize all of the tools that are available-Science based selection programs, Internet searches, volunteer activities, and job shadowing. Thorough preparation helps guarantee success.

One more set of startling statistics before we move on:

- 20% dropped out in the 1960s
- 33% dropped out in the 1990s
- 50% dropped out in 2006
- 52% now drop out or transfer by the first year

More than ever careful selection is critical to college success. I'll go into greater depth on positioning your student in order to capture the attention of those schools that will be a great fit in the chapter Setting Yourself Apart.

For more information regarding the Selection process go to:
www.collegewithoutstudentloans.com/selection.html

Chapter 3

# ACCEPTANCE

Although the final acceptance or rejection decision is ultimately made by the institution knowing and then utilizing some of the selection criteria can put your student at the top of the stack.

**It is vital to replace the common mindset of "How can my student compete?" with "Which colleges are willing to compete for my student?" Let's change the paradigm.**

While a central part of the admission process is to know which colleges your student prefers you can take it a step further and apply to colleges of equal quality that compete for the same type of students. Our research center can direct you to these "unknown" colleges that will provide award letters that your student can use as leverage. Success in the admission process includes going to a college that meets a high percentage of your student's financial need and a well-defined and encompassing admission strategy will help you achieve the success you deserve.

Test scores and GPAs are just starting points or the common denominator among applicants. We will now touch on tagging, legacies, and demonstrable interest.

## Tagging

A "Tag" is a positive mark added to a student's admissions application to indicate that he or she is of special interest to the college. Children of alumni get tags known as "legacies," the size of their tag or perhaps we should say the size of their advantage is usually measured by the depth of the parent's generosity to the school.

Students with special talents also get tagged. For example, students with outstanding academic achievements, athletic qualities, or musically/artistically inclined students get tagged for special interest to the colleges.

Your student's intended school may need three tuba players for the marching band and have a glut of saxophone players. This may not help your saxophone-playing student but be aware that sometimes it's just enough of an advantage to help them get in at competing equally attractive institutions. Having more than one school choice gives your student an advantage because the other school just may need another saxophone player.

Underrepresented minorities, underrepresented sexes, and students from underrepresented states receive tags. Based on Federal requirements for funding your student may receive a tag if they are from a certain state, or male, etc.

During the admission process your student may become aware of schools that are seeking to diversify their student population. Again, like the saxophone player, some schools will need them and some may not.

Once an application is tagged the individual is removed from the common pool of applicants and is moved to an entirely new level for special consideration. An applicant that normally may not have been looked at twice based on GPA may find that being tagged opens many doors. It's vitally important to know in advance which colleges give extra attention to which specific tags.

## Packaging

Imagine looking out over a cornfield. There are thousands and thousands of stalks of corn all planted in neat evenly spaced rows. You've seen the pictures or perhaps you grew up around a corn farm. Now imagine that several of these stalks of corn are three feet taller than all of the rest.

It's pretty easy to see how they differ from the remaining stalks isn't it? Help your student stand out like those taller corn stalks amid all of the freshman applicants and you make the job of the admissions officer easier in selecting your student.

The key to making your student one of the "wanted ones" is by promoting their value to each school. College is big business with an abundance of rules and procedures geared to fill their classrooms with students that have a high probability of success. Make it obvious to them that your student is the one candidate that they have been looking for and that selecting your child for acceptance is going to be a big win for them.

How does your student set themselves apart from all the other applicants? You must "Package & Position" your student based upon the College Acceptance Profile (CAP) that is unique to each school. The applicants with the highest CAP scores are the most attractive to colleges and are eligible for the best financial aid packages. These students receive more grants and free money rather than them having to obtain student loans and participate in work-study programs.

The CAP criteria used by selective and elite institutions includes:

- Awards-National, Regional, State, County, and School
- Academics-Standard Test Scores
- Activities-School & Outside (Leadership is Important)
- Community Service-Volunteerism, Helping Others
- Character Traits-Teacher/Counselor Ratings

The key to gaining acceptance is promoting your student based upon these evaluation points. **Admissions committees rely on CAP scores to objectively review each applicant and then compare them to the established selection criteria for that school.**

Your student's living college profile is a continuing work-in-progress of creating their marketability to colleges. During their college years the living profile is a platform that your student can use as a guide for the rest of their life and will help ensure success no matter what goals or desires they wish to accomplish. For parents who realize the importance of this one area and begin working on it early on it is their opportunity to establish those life strategy patterns within their student while he or she is in junior high or middle school. Their college profile becomes their resume of achievement that colleges and future employers will use to judge and rank them.

The living profile is the starting point for most college admissions. Most people have been led to believe that the key to getting accepted into college are GPA and SAT or ACT scores. Those do play an important role but community service and extracurricular activities help the college determine whether or not there is a reasonable probability that the student can be academically successful upon attending.

Remember that they are looking for a student that will be a good investment; one who demonstrates a high probability of success in terms of completion, career, and who ultimately will give back to their alma mater through endowments. The high success rate of their student body also allows the college to increase the costs associated with attending their school.

## So why don't colleges just take anyone willing to pay their fees?

They don't want to mislead students into believing that they can be successful at their university if the available information they have about the applicant indicates otherwise. Also they don't want to create a trend of drawn out degrees (the seven-year plan) or a trend of students that fail to graduate.

Schools also assume that the applicant probably isn't very interested in attending a school where their chance of success is poor. Everyone's goal, including the university's, is to make good decisions that will help everyone be successful.

If the college realizes that your student is a good fit they will find a way to get them. In a survey by the National Association of College Admission Counselors 54% of the colleges that responded said that they use preferential packaging.

With that in mind let's look at the components of most admission applications. Five critically important areas on the application are:

- High school classes attended.
- Grades received in those classes.
- Cumulative GPA-both weighted and non-weighted.
- SAT and/or ACT scores.
- Essay.

Let's assume that your student's peer's GPA and test scores are comparable to their own. This is where the essay comes into play. For many schools the essay writing makes up nearly half of the admissions scoring.

## What is the essay for?

Life in school is interesting and challenging with algebraic equations, Bunsen burners, sentence diagrams, etc., but most students have commitments outside of school as well. The good news is that colleges pay attention to life inside and outside the classroom. These extra activities actually reveal a great deal about your student and as noted above, an important part of the admission process.

Depending on the application questions the underlying answer colleges want is how your student's interests and activities will contribute to their academic and career success. Keep these questions in mind during the essay process:

- How has the student made a meaningful contribution to someone/something?
- What are the student's non-academic interests?
- Has the student maintained a long-term commitment?
- Can the student manage their time and priorities?
- What diversity would the student bring to the student body?

"We're looking for a commitment to and a passion for an activity outside of the academic setting-we're looking for depth rather than breadth," explains Nanci Tessier, a college admissions director.

Colleges do not have a checklist of requirements when it comes to extracurricular activities but what they want to see is individuality and consistent commitment. When they see a student that has contributed to their community they believe that that will translate into a contribution to their school-now and in the future.

## School Activities

Encourage your student to get involved early in their school years by letting them explore and by helping them decide how much and what to do. Two examples are writing for the school paper and or volunteering on campus. You'll need to ensure that they can give 100% in each activity while maintaining their academics. Two things to keep in mind:

- Don't worry about being president or captain. The key is doing something significant regardless if it's center stage or behind the scenes.
- Non-traditional or mature activities (MAs) also get attention. We will cover MAs in more depth later.

## Work Experience

Work experience whether paid or volunteer, year-round, or summer can help your student identify career interests and goals, gain work experience, and apply classroom learning to the real world. It's also a great way to earn money for college of course.

Encourage your student to shadow someone at his or her job or to apply for an internship at a local company to gain additional experience. Working outside the traditional fast food or babysitting jobs displays maturity and career mindedness and demonstrates to colleges that the student is focused on a successful college outcome.

## The Essay Process

Keep in mind that admission officers utilize the essay to determine and evaluate the student's ability to effectively write and communicate their ideas while learning more about the student. Many colleges will provide specific topics while others leave the topics wide open. Regardless of whether it's a canned question or an open topic refer to the above points on how your student can communicate their involvement, meaningful contributions, and aspirations through the essay.

## Student Essay Guideline

- Showcase your writing ability while demonstrating your personality and passion through your writing.
- Be opinionated. Even without an ideal topic let how you feel about the subject come through. The reader should know more about you when they finish reading your essay.
- Incorporate your ideas and opinions about your insight into the essay, your qualities, your interest in and passion regarding the subject. Be honest and show your true reaction to the subject matter. Use the opportunity to show how much you care and why you feel the way that you do.

- If given the opportunity to choose the topic write about a specific event or an activity that you feel strongly about.

- It is an accepted practice to avoid general topics such as world events, religious affiliation, and philosophic stances.

- Your writing approach should be interesting and demonstrate maturity.

- Wherever possible highlight examples of leadership, vision, and situations where you have overcome adversity or challenging circumstances.

- Convey your dedication to and your ability to have a sustained commitment to goals and emphasize your ability to complete tasks. Demonstrate your self-dependence.

- Be concise, clear, direct, and to the point while writing with conviction.

- Check your punctuation and spelling. Have your essay proof-read by a qualified individual such as a teacher or professional essay reviewer.

- Don't repeat your ideas without expanding upon them.

- Never go beyond the required length of the essay.

- Communicate as you normally would and do not use large or difficult words in an effort to impress your reader.

- Do not use exclamation points. Rewrite until you convey the thought with the desired emphasis.

- Vary your language and avoid repeating a word or variation of the same word when describing something.

Once the essay is complete solicit some unbiased opinions prior to submitting it to the college. Counselors, a favorite teacher, or mentor can offer a helpful critique. It's critical however that the essay not appear professionally prepared. Be wary of any college assistance firm that offers to prepare an essay for your student. As with all components of your student's application the college wants to see the student demonstrate their own abilities and interests.

For more information on Acceptance go to:
www.collegewithoutstudentloans.com/acceptance.html

# Chapter 4

# FINANCIAL AID

F inancial Aid-It's not what you think
College costs
money…whether it's
your money, the government's
money, or the school's money
depends on an effective
strategy and a winning
formula. Since my goal is to

help your student attend a great school without student loans, aka "Free Money," this chapter will help you understand the definition of needs-based financial aid. Even if you don't think you'll be eligible for it omitting this step in the college funding process could cost you dearly. Many schools won't even consider your student for "non-need" based aid if you don't try applying for need-based aid.

Financial aid can be made up of these sources:

*Mary and Ted were both working professionals, owned their own home, had investments, and an average retirement plan. They also had two children entering high school. The thought of providing college for their children filled them with dread and discouragement rather than excitement about the possibilities. Why? They immediately dismissed the notion that their children would receive financial aid for school since they considered themselves a middle-income family. They equated financial aid with being needy and quickly disqualified themselves as being eligible for financial aid.*

*Once I sat down with them to get a clearer picture of both their finances and the options available to them they began to see the exciting future and opportunities that awaited their two bright and motivated children.*

The Higher Education Act of 1965 states that it is the parent's responsibility to educate their children beyond the 12th grade. Most importantly the law states that if a family can demonstrate "Need" the government will assist in paying for the education.

The good news is that "Need" is not subjective but is based on a formula and you can estimate your contribution much easier by understanding the calculation.

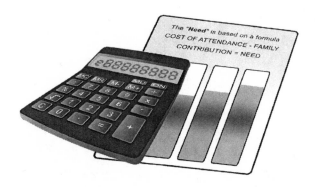

The "Need" is based on a formula
COST OF ATTENDANCE - FAMILY
CONTRIBUTION = NEED

## Cost of Attendance

The financial aid administrator at each school develops the average Cost of Attendance (COA) for different categories of students. Some programs may have lab fees or higher charges for books and supplies than other programs. Students living off campus may have higher room and board costs and additional transportation expenses compared to students living on campus.

Many families only consider the cost of tuition and don't take into account the expenses that aren't covered by financial aid. Everything from ramen noodles to bus or plane tickets home are part of your student's COA. Sororities and fraternities, intramural sports, and other activities surprise many families with additional college expenses.

For Federal Student Aid programs the financial administrator must use the definition of COA given in the financial aid law. That law specifies that the COA include tuition, fees, and an allowance for living expenses such as room and board, plus books, supplies, and transportation costs. The law also provides limited allowances for handicapped students.

The COA can vary for each student at the same school but students in the same situation must have the same COA.

## Family Contribution

The next part of the formula is the family contribution. It is determined by the need analysis methodology prescribed by law for use in calculating a student's Expected Family Contribution. (EFC)

The EFC is the amount you as a family are expected to contribute toward your student's educational expenses during the academic year. This is recalculated each year your student attends school. The Free Application for Federal Student Aid (FAFSA) is used to calculate your EFC.

For dependent students your family contribution is the sum of four separate calculations: the contribution from parents' income; the contribution from parents' assets; the contribution from student's income; and the contribution from student's assets.

Completing a FAFSA on your own is daunting at best. Working with a professional who understands how EFC is calculated is the key in maximizing your position to benefit from needs-based financial aid.

The analogy I like to use is this: Imagine if the IRS asked you to file all the information on your tax form without you having any way of knowing what you were going to pay or without any way of knowing the strategies that you could use to lower your tax bite. In this situation you would probably want to seek the advice of someone who knows the rules of the game. In the same way seeking a knowledgeable source for completing the FAFSA and Profile aid applications improves your position.

### Need

After subtracting your EFC from the college's COA the remainder is **need**. Your family contribution will be the same for every college but your need at each college will vary according to the college's overall cost.

For instance, if your EFC is $10,000 it would be the same whether your student attends a school that is $13,000 a year or an elite school that is $43,000 a year. The need varies but your contribution remains the same. **Why not choose the $43,000 a year school if it's a good fit for your student instead of thinking the $13,000 a year school is all you can afford?**

There are a growing number of colleges that fill only a set percentage of each student's demonstrated need. For example at a school that fills 90% of need a student that demonstrates $10,000 in need would only receive $9,000 in financial aid. At these colleges it is even more important that you have taken the very important first step of seeking out knowledge about how the financial aid process works and how to improve your situation. After all 90% of $10,000 is much better than 90% of $5,000.

### Applying for Aid

At nearly every workshop I conduct I'm asked: "Why should I seek assistance in filling out the FAFSA?"

The FAFSA form is rather intimidating for most families as it contains over 100 questions that range from the number of people in the household to EFC. It's no wonder that many make mistakes while others don't even file believing that they earn too much to qualify. College tuition and fees increased 439% from 1982 to 2007 (25 years) while the median family income only increased 147%.

The Federal government reports consistently that at least 78% of submitted forms contain errors. Just one mistake on the FAFSA can add thousands of dollars to your EFC.

If job loss, home foreclosure, or other financial event prevents you from making any contribution to your child's education it may be that you can claim zero as your EFC. If your adjusted gross income is less than $50,000 and your current assets are less than the allowable limit your expected contribution can be zero as well.

While you need numbers from your most recent tax return assets aren't part of that and need to be included on the FAFSA. It includes the income and assets of both the parents AND the student. The new filing period online is the first business day in January and continues through March 30th each year for incoming freshmen.

FAFSA is submitted online at: www.fafsa.ed.gov. Always keep copies of all the forms you submit as part of the financial aid process.

This will help you keep track of what you have done and makes it easy to resubmit required information if a form is lost. If you miss the deadline it is assumed that the student will not file the FAFSA and may not be eligible for merit-based as well as need-based aid. Keep in touch with the financial aid office as most problems arise when deadlines are missed. It's better to call the school a few times too often rather than miss their deadline.

*This is what happened when Kathy and Rick Sims submitted the FAFSA for their daughter Brittany. After being accepted to her top school choice they were told that they weren't eligible for any financial aid. The Sims begrudgingly accepted the fact that they were going to have to pay 100% of the COA of $24,356 annually.*

*Six months later Brittany left home to attend college and her mother attended my "College Without Student Loans" workshop hoping to find assistance for her son Kent. He would attend college in 24 months and she knew their resources would not cover the expense of two full time college students. During this workshop she learned that professional assistance could be the answer to their financial dilemma.*

*Though they believed it was too late to get funding for Brittany, Kathy and Rick contracted with my firm to develop a plan for Kent's college expenses. While reviewing the data submitted for Brittany I discovered two errors in the FAFSA. Immediately I had the family appeal to Brittany's school financial aid office to accept the results of the corrected FAFSA.*

*To the Sims' surprise the school reviewed the appeal and the corrected EFC was lowered to a point that Brittany was eligible to receive a total of $12,850 annually from Federal and State*

*assistance. Rick said the decision to contract my firm's services was the best investment he made the entire year. With our assistance their two children were able to attend the schools of their dreams and the Sims saved nearly $150,000. This is REAL money that Rick and Kathy are now putting toward their retirement.*

## Your Financial Aid Timeline:

- Indicate the college(s) you want the results of the FAFSA sent to. When filing online you are required to give the correct college identification code.

- When the analysis is complete the information is electronically sent to the colleges.

- Contact the college aid office in March to confirm they received all of the information they need to consider you for local or state aid. You may need to provide more information so be sure to send it in promptly.

- You will receive an aid offer via a summary statement called Student Aid Report (SAR) typically between March 15th and April 15th.

- Review it carefully and follow the instructions closely to correct any errors. Hand deliver it or mail the original SAR and a copy of the corrected SAR to the financial aid office of the college you are interested in attending.

- The college will compile a financial aid package containing the types of aid it can offer each student based on the SAR information.

- If accepting the offer you must sign the award letter and return it to the college by May 1st. If you decide to reject the offer let the school know immediately so the school can make an offer to other applicants.
- The school will send you any additional applications it needs to process your request.
- If your family financial situation changes during the year and more or less financial aid is needed inform the financial aid office. You will have to provide additional documentation to receive more aid but schools may be able to provide more money. It's certainly worth the time and effort to ask.

For more information regarding financial aid go to: www.collegewithoutstudentloans.com/financialaid.html

# Chapter 5

# FEDERAL FINANCIAL AID
# PROGRAM DEFINED

F ederal student aid programs are the number one way
that students get the financial help that will allow them
to attend college. Completing the FAFSA is required in
order to demonstrate eligibility for Federal programs. Here are
the more popular financial aid programs:

### Federal Pell Grant

For many students this is the foundation for financial aid. It is
the government's largest grant program in terms of cost and is
for undergraduates only. It is presumed to be the first source of
aid to the student; therefore it does not consider other sources of

aid, in fact, other aid can be added on after the Pell Grant. EFC Methodology determines the amount of a Pell Grant award. A grant decreases in relation to EFC so that together the grant and the family contribution do not exceed the COA. The maximum Pell Grant award for the 2012-2013 academic year is $5,833.

## Federal Supplemental Educational Opportunity Grant (SEOG)

This is a grant to help first-time undergraduates with exceptional financial need as determined by the school. Students may receive up to $4,000 per year with a minimum grant of $100. It allows for an additional $400 for students in study-abroad programs that are more expensive than their college costs. There is no aggregate limit on the amount of SEOG that can be received.

*When I met Eric and Brandy they had been married five years and were raising son Brian, from a previous marriage, with joint custody. During Brian's senior year of high school Eric went online and completed the FAFSA form to the best of his ability.*

*He thought it was just another of the many forms that needed to be filled out for college. During a "College Night" presentation at the high school a counselor told the audience that the FAFSA was "Free" and simple to fill out. The counselor emphasized that it was a simple form each parent could fill out themselves and that they would not need to engage a professional for help with this task.*

Based upon Eric and Brandy's income, assets, and retirement accounts listed in the FAFSA form resulted in an Expected Family Contribution (EFC) of $47,325 per year. This calculation meant that Brian would not be eligible for any state or federal grants to reduce the cost of college. Based upon the information provided by the public high school and other parents, Eric and Brandy were not prepared to pay the full cost of college.

Eric called me in a panic in order to determine how the family EFC could be reduced; otherwise Brian could not attend one of his dream schools. When we met I found several common mistakes that parents make when they fill out the FAFSA.

- Brian spent over 50% of the year with his biological mother who had not re-married and whose sole income was significantly less than Eric's.
- Eric was told that the father's income had to be calculated.
- Eric listed his total retirement accounts value as current assets.
- Biological mother (Debra) had no retirement accounts and little assets.

When the FAFSA was correctly re-calculated using only Debra's financial data and not Eric and Brandy's, the result was a new EFC of $5,948. The reduction in EFC of over $40,000 annually positioned Brian for both federal and state grants. The cost savings *by submitting the corrected FAFSA was $67,000. According to estimates by the Federal government, costly mistakes like these occur in over 80% of FAFSA forms submitted each year.*

|  | *Eric's FAFSA* | *Debra's FAFSA* |
|---|---|---|
| *EFC* | *047,325* | *005,948* |
| *Federal Grants* | $ 0/yr. | $4,000/yr. |
| *State Grants* | $ 0/yr. | $9,500/yr. |
|  |  |  |
| *"Free" Money* | $ 0/yr. | $13,400/yr. |
| *Years of College* | x 5 | x 5 |
| **Total Savings** | **$ 0** | **$67,000** |

## Federal Work-Study Program

The college will make a job available for an undergraduate student, paid by the hour for a minimum of at least the current Federal minimum wage. The job may be on or off campus and students must be paid at least once a month. Students cannot earn more than $300 above their total Work-Study award.

## Federal Direct Perkins Loan

This is the first of the loan programs with very favorable terms. The amount students may borrow depends on the institution they attend. At institutions with low default rates (below 15%) and the approval of the Secretary of Education students may borrow more than at other institutions. An annual limit for undergraduate students is $5,500 and $8,000 for graduate students. Cumulative limits for undergraduate students are $27,500 and $60,000 for graduate students.

The Federal government pays the interest (currently 5%) on the loan while students have at least half-time status and for nine months after graduation or nine months after dropping below half-time status. If students enter their grace period and then re-enter school before the grace period expires they receive a new complete grace period when they again enter less than half-time status. Students have up to ten years to repay the loan.

## Federal Direct Loan
## (AKA Subsidized Stafford Loans)

These are low interest loans made to students with at least half-time status. The Federal government pays the interest on the loan until the loan enters its repayment phase. Direct Loans are made by the Department of Education by way of the individual colleges. The Direct Loan is an entitlement and therefore anyone and everyone who qualifies will receive it. New Direct Loans in the 2012-2013 academic year have a fixed rate of 6.8%.

## Federal Unsubsidized Direct Loan
## (AKA Stafford Loans)

This is where we start to enter dangerous waters. The Unsubsidized Federal Direct Loan has the same loan limits as the need-based

Direct Loans but the government does NOT pay the interest while borrowers are in college.

A student may receive an Unsubsidized Direct Loan even if they do not demonstrate financial need. While the unsubsidized loan cannot exceed the student's COA minus other aid it essentially is allowed to replace a student's EFC.

A Direct Loan is unsubsidized when the student is responsible for the interest that accumulates while the student is enrolled in school. Only loan principal is deferred for the Unsubsidized Direct Loan. That means that interest payments must be made during the in-school period, the grace period, and during periods of deferment. Another option is to allow the interest to accrue and be capitalized and added to the loan principal when payment begins thus increasing the principal. Unsubsidized Stafford Loan charges the student 6.8% interest from day one. It is possible for a student to qualify for a combination of subsidized and unsubsidized loans. For example a first year student receiving a $3,500 need-based Direct Loan could also receive a $2,000 unsubsidized loan.

### Federal Direct Parent Loans for Undergraduate Students (Direct PLUS Loan)

This program allows parents to borrow money to cover any costs not already covered by the student's financial aid package, up to the full cost of attendance. There is no cumulative limit and currently Direct PLUS Loans have a fixed interest rate of 7.9%. If you have been paying attention however, you know that I'm not a fan of you footing the bill for your student's education. Wise positioning and planning can pay huge dividends in securing offers to desirable schools with little cash contribution from you as parents. Remember this is **College WITHOUT Student Loans**.

## Tax Provisions

There are provisions in the tax code to allow for deductions and tax credits tied to your student's education. Fees and Tuition are allowed a maximum deduction per student per year of $4,000. Another option is the American Opportunity Tax Credit and the Lifetime Learning Tax Credit although you cannot take both the Tuition and Fees Deduction and either the American Tax Credit of Lifetime Learning Tax Credit for the same student in the same tax year.

## Planning Ahead

As I wrap up this chapter with information on the Section 529 Savings Plan many readers will find this to be information that is too little too late. If you have very young children however, grand children, or know of those about to be parents, passing this book and this information on to them could be better than any wind-up toy or baby blanket as a gift.

Section 529 Savings plans are Federal tax-exempt college saving vehicles that allow participants to save money in a special college savings account on behalf of a designated beneficiary for qualified higher education expenses. Most states exempt earnings from state income tax and some states allow families to deduct the full or partial amount of their contribution from their state income tax.

The Section 529 Savings Plan is treated as an asset of the account owner and not the beneficiary. If a parent owns the Section 529 Savings Plan the value is included in the EFC. If grandparents own the Section 529 Savings Plan none of the value is included. A Section 529 Savings Plan owned by a dependent student or by a trust or custodian for the student is counted as an asset of the parent.

## 529 Prepaid Tuition Plans

Section 529 Tuition Prepayment plans are no longer treated as an available student resource in the Federal needs analysis formula when determining eligibility for financial aid. Under the Higher Education Reconciliation Act of 2005 they are treated the same as a Section 529 Savings Plan.

The Section 529 Tuition Prepayment plan is treated as an asset of the account owner and not the beneficiary. If a parent owns the Section 529 Tuition Prepayment plan the value is included in the EFC while none of the value is included if it is owned by grandparents. Like the Section 529 Savings Plan, if owned by a dependent student, a trust, or custodian for the student the Tuition Prepayment Plan is counted as an asset of the parent.

## Coverdell Education Savings Account

A Coverdell Education Savings Account (ESA) is a trust created exclusively for paying the qualified higher education expenses of the designated beneficiary. Tax-free withdrawals from a Coverdell ESA can be used to pay for qualifying elementary and secondary school expenses including expenses at private schools.

The maximum contribution amount is $2,000 per beneficiary from all sources per year. Contributions are phased out for incomes ranging between $95,000 and $110,000 (single filers) or $190,000 and $220,000 (married filing jointly). Contributions are not deductible on Federal or state income tax but earnings accumulate tax-free. Qualified distributions are exempt from Federal income tax and are not counted as income on the FAFSA and thus do not reduce financial aid eligibility.

The Coverdell ESA is treated as an asset of the account owner and not the beneficiary. If a parent owns the Coverdell ESA the value is included in the EFC. If grandparents own the account none of the value is included. A Coverdell ESA owned by a dependent student or by a trust or custodian for the student is not counted as the student's asset.

## Change-and how it affects many

New rules and regulations are constantly being discussed for these programs in Washington, D.C. Recent university reports indicate that over 82% of attendees are participating in the Federal loan program today.

The vast majority of students today are taking on debt to pay for their college education. Figures are on the rise but it is currently estimated that student loan debt tops the $1 trillion mark. It is an economic bubble that is about to burst which will result in a major economic downturn.

Now you understand why *College Without Student Loans* is such a critical read for every family of college bound children.

For updated information about Federal Aid programs go to:
www.collegewithoutstudentloans.com/federalaid.html

Chapter 6

# WHERE'S THE MONEY?

"A fool with a plan is better than a genius with none."
**—T. Boone Pickens**, July 2000

Once your student has filed the FAFSA the doors open to exploring various financial aid opportunities that can make the difference between affordability of your student's first choice school or having to settle for less. This is the money that most parents don't realize that schools are ready and eager to extend to the students they want to fill their classrooms with.

It has been estimated that an excess of $60 billion is available every year that goes untouched by students.

In most cases parents assume that "Scholarships" are the key to making up the financial difference for them. Scholarships are monies distributed by entities such as civic organizations like Rotary or Lions, or through corporations. These funds are paid directly to the student to offset the cost of college. They represent less than 3% of total money available for education, however. A college plan that pays the majority of the costs by scholarships is an ill-fated strategy that will have disastrous results for most families.

Something that most people don't realize about scholarships is the effect they can have on the merit-based aid packages offered from schools. Even though selective and elite schools may offer attractive packages as an enticement to your student it is essentially a discount. Prior to attending classes each semester they will often require your student to declare any scholarship funds that they have been awarded. In essence the school will see that as money that they don't have to provide in order for your student to attend.

As an example, if your student has been offered $20,000 in a merit-based award and the local Rotary provides them with a $3,500 scholarship you may think that they now have $23,500 in funds to attend school. The school however, will see the $3,500 as an amount that they no longer have to discount from their fees and amend their offer to $16,500.

Before becoming discouraged keep in mind that scholarships can be a great asset if your student is heading to a state school. If that is the case our advice is to get the best grades, best test scores, and as many scholarships as possible because that is the only way you are going to afford college other than by taking on student debt.

As we will discuss in the following chapter, Setting Yourself Apart, the mature aspects of your student are the ones that universities will notice and offer financial aid awards for in the form of merit-based aid.

Merit-based aid is an incentive used to attract students considered valuable to the institution in the "subjective" areas of academics, arts, athletics, and activities. Merit awards are distributed by the Admissions Office of each school in the form of discounts subsidized by endowment funds. Colleges control over $150 billion in endowment funds, the 2nd largest pool of money behind Federal Aid, meaning that the college gets to choose who gets this money. Properly positioning and demonstrating the value of your student is not just a good idea but imperative if you want to make their college education affordable today.

Private schools generally fashion the highest COA, or list price, and many families eliminate them immediately because they believe that they cannot afford the higher expense. While this seems reasonable on the surface it is actually faulty thinking. Private institutions have the largest endowment funds and therefore offer the largest merit awards or discounts to the students that meet or exceed the school's admission criteria. It's just another reason not to rule out a private school.

It is reported today that 46 states are experiencing budget deficits and each one of them is cutting back on educational subsidies. Where's the money to make college affordable to most students?

It's not at state funded schools. Private universities and colleges, which most people assume are too expensive, have the funds to extend the most attractive offers to students who fit their profile. Accessing this additional money at selective and elite schools may require a bit more effort as nearly 250 schools now require the College Scholarship Service (CSS) profile but it is well worth it.

While filing the FAFSA is free, and submitted to the Department of Education, the CSS requires an additional charge per school and is submitted through collegeboard.org. It also involves a more detailed account of your financial profile for the previous two years. The FAFSA only requires basic information for the past year so planning ahead and positioning is absolutely critical.

Since merit awards are based on subjective criteria schools use the CSS Profile to help them determine how they will distribute financial aid.

**Did I mention that college today is Big Business?**
Now that you are armed with the financial facts I challenge
you to change your perception that a college education
automatically means student loans and attending the local
community college.

The keys to properly position your student are having them
achieve strong SAT/ACT scores, maintain contact with the
Admissions Department Chairman at their selected schools, and

to demonstrate their direction, focus, and the other qualities their potential schools are looking for.

Students who are in the top 25% of the incoming freshman class often get preferential treatment. Researching the SAT/ACT scores for incoming freshman will give you a good idea of where your student needs to rank. Encourage your student to apply to schools where they rank above the median or average student and the schools will respond with more attractive financial aid packages.

Students that take advanced high school classes can test out of some entry-level college classes by passing CLEP (College Level Examination Program) tests. This can save time and money. Investigate advance placement classes and those that offer college credit while in high school when your student begins their high school career. **This increases the desirability of your student to many schools.**

Another way to maximize your student's financial aid award is to choose colleges that have the best histories of giving generous financial aid packages. During the selection process make sure you completely research the type and amount of merit-based aid that each school reportedly offered to average students.

A school's financial aid package is not set in stone. It is possible to leverage a more favorable outcome than your student's initial offer. This is where knowing your EFC and the school's history of financial aid can give you an accurate idea of what you should have received.

Mistakes can and do occur. If the school's offer seems off ask the school to reconsider the offer. I have seen many cases where schools gave $2,000, $3,000, and even $4,000 more than they originally offered. Asking for a review in the appropriate manner can result in an increase of thousands of dollars if an error was made in processing. The school wants your student to attend so they will want to make it right.

*John came to my office and presented his daughter's Student Aid Report (SAR) from a prestigious university that outlined an offer of 29% Gift (free) money and 81% Self Help (loans) money. He was a proud father with what he believed was a great offer. After all, his daughter was given "free" money. After researching the school I discovered a potential mistake because on average 81% in free or gift money was typically offered. I had John send a letter to the school requesting a review of their original offer. One week later he walked back into my office with a new SAR that reflected an increased offer of $23,500 per year which equated to a total of $95,000 over the course of four years.*

*It was no wonder that John could not stop smiling because this additional award made his daughter's TOP school choice affordable within his college budget.*

Once again College Without Student Loans was able to help someone by doing a little homework. Reports published recently demonstrate that a college education is still a wise investment even if student loans are required to obtain it.

Estimated lifetime incomes of those without a college degree are around $600,000 compared to averages in excess of $1.3 million for a graduate with a Bachelor's degree.

Parent's debt to fund their students' education rose to over $100 billion in 2011 which is an absolutely terrifying statistic. As we've demonstrated there are multiple avenues and funding options available to you and your odds of accessing them increase greatly with a team of experts on your side.

A misunderstanding of the methodology schools use for financial aid coupled with a lack of planning force many families to turn to loans in order to fund their children's education. It is critical to develop a plan long before it's time to send them off to college.

It is my personal prediction that student loans will continue to grow faster than college costs are rising simply because it's so easy to get the loan. Ultimately the student becomes an indentured servant to the Federal government, the supervisor and overseer of student loans.

As SARs begin to arrive review them carefully and look at the big picture. A $10,000 award may cover all of your need at one school but may leave you short at another. Choose wisely. Pay close attention to special conditions or requirements that may also be a part of the financial aid package such as maintaining a certain GPA or only attending classes within a certain major.

While I've highlighted several strategies to maximize your education dollars it's important to keep in mind that in the end the ideal college for your student is the one that fits them the best. Cost should not be the only factor that drives your student's college decision.

*Mary and Don attended one of my parent workshops and requested a private consultation to discuss their particular situation regarding their two daughters. Don was a successful corporate financial officer for a local company and Mary worked part time as an interior designer. Mary's main focus was on the two girls. Terri, the oldest, was entering her junior year of high school and was very focused on athletics. Sara, two years younger, was very social and keenly focused on academics, while adding community service projects in her free time.*

*When we met, Don emphasized that his main priority was that both girls be able to choose their own direction in life. This was very personal because Don's parents put great pressure on him to follow the professional family trend and become a dentist. He attended a prestigious university suggested by his father with a pre-dental major. Much to his father's chagrin, when the time came for Don to enter dental school, not enjoying the dental arena, he opted out and went into business.*

*Terri was a highly acclaimed softball player and played nearly year round for both traveling and high school teams. Don's hope was for his daughter to earn a "Full Ride" scholarship in softball which would ease the financial strain of saving for college. The expenses to keep Terri playing softball were extremely great and took away any hope of extra savings for college.*

*My first objective for Mary and Don was to set realistic expectations, and unfortunately I had to burst their belief that a "Full Ride" scholarship was a possibility. Since title IX came into effect, creating equality of money spent on women and men's athletics, the NCAA governs sports differently. The net effect is that coaches (276 Division I) have a set amount of full scholarships (12) to field their team of 30+ players. Based upon the facts today most full scholarships are typically divided up 25% to 50% per athlete. The most lucrative Division I sports of Men's Football, Men's Basketball, and Women's Basketball, do not offer many, if any, "Full Ride" scholarships.*

*Once these facts were absorbed, Mary and Don began to ask why interest by college coaches only came from introductions made by the coach of Terri's travelling team. The answer was that the only person promoting Terri was her coach and he knew a few select coaches on a friendly basis. Approaching coaches on an "Athlete First, Student Second" basis will only work for the elite athletes desiring to attend Division I schools.*

*I suggested that they change their paradigm/thinking to "Student First, Athlete Second" with the schools that were a great*

*"Fit" for Terri. We then contacted the business school chairpersons and softball coaches at eight specific schools and promoted Terri as an excellent "Student Athlete". Terri was accepted for admission at all eight schools based on her academic records and community service achievements. In April she received Student Aid Reports (SAR) that ranged from a 40% to an 85% discount for her Cost of Attendance (COA).*

*Terri is now attending a prestigious eastern U.S. Division I university that offered her a 75% "Free Money" (discount) off their published COA of $52,000. Because this offer is based on her academic and community service achievements, even if she becomes hurt and can no longer play softball the "Free Money" award will be maintained as long as Terri completes a minimum of 12 units per semester and maintains a 3.0 g.p.a. If it was only an athletic scholarship and she got hurt and could not compete any longer, the scholarship would be revoked.*

*My experience is that there is always more "Free Money" available for good students versus good athletes. I know firsthand because my athletic scholarship was taken away after I got hurt. I then wised up and got an academic scholarship in order to continue my education.*

Establishing an effective plan for college is a "must have." If you need help then employ an expert to assist you just like you would search out assistance from an attorney for legal matters or a dentist for issues with your teeth. In the end it's doing whatever it takes to guarantee a successful outcome in securing your student's college education.

For more information on where the money is, go to:
www.collegewithoutstudentloans.com/funding.html

# Chapter 7

# SET YOURSELF APART

There are methods and techniques when implemented correctly will have colleges wanting your student to attend their institution. In this chapter I'll reveal the ins and outs of how your student can effectively set themselves apart from the others competing for admission. Being unique or different gives your student a competitive edge.

It may appear that a prospective student is asking for the privilege of attending an institution during the college search process but the fact is that they are in more control than one might think.

How does one begin to compete against others with higher GPAs and test scores? The answer is....MAs. I'm not talking about the degree. An "MA" is mature activity that demonstrates adult behavior to the college decision makers that your student interfaces with during the admissions process. As a demographic most high school students are lumped into the category of pizza eating video game-playing teenagers.

While it is unfair to paint that kind of a picture many of the admissions decision makers at colleges start the process that way. To get a competitive edge your student's MA will set them apart and get them noticed in a positive light.

High school activities such as volunteering for yearbook, playing in the band, and participating in sports are typical school activities and are expected of above-average students. These are not bad things to do but demonstrating MA is engaging in activities or interests that people associate with adults. Being on the school newspaper staff is typical while serving as the Editor of the newspaper is better. Developing a highly successful advertising campaign, writing a marketing plan, and plotting the return on investment is the MA or best way to be part of the staff.

If your student has an interest in entomology, stamp collecting, raising homing pigeons or even quilting, these are activities where high school students don't commonly invest time or energy. Discuss ways that your student can elevate their current activities to MA status or they can explore new interests in local government or green initiatives. Starting a business or charity is another MA.

Babysitting is a typical high school job but creating a service company with an established database of available sitters, individual qualifications, and safety certification while developing marketing and advertising to offer reliable babysitters in the area is an MA that will get schools to take notice. **Displaying entrepreneurial initiatives are viewed positively by admissions officers in the more competitive and selective schools.**

The student that transforms their interests into a passionate endeavor may reveal that through their essays and submitted college applications. They should connect those interests with real-life skills such as research, categorizing, and follow-through which demonstrate that they are the type of person that will overcome unforeseen challenges in order to accomplish their goals. The tenacity to achieve is a winning attribute for elite schools because it demonstrates that your student won't give up in the face of adversity.

If your student becomes passionate about starting a business they will want to consider which schools appreciate students with entrepreneurial vision. If they enjoy the research and cataloging involved in collecting anything there are different schools that value those interests.

Every college has their own DNA. Some colleges want brainiac students, some want above-average students with strong civic service aptitudes, while others may focus on those with strong leadership experiences. When your student's interests align with the college's DNA the school will consider them a sound investment.

Suddenly GPA, test scores, and other standards begin to fade in comparison with the MAs and the potential achievement that individual students display.

How can you discover each college's DNA as you and your student begin to look beneath the surface of the colorful brochures and canned presentations? What is each school looking for? It's time to start asking questions. Each student has unique interests, skills, and potential that translates to their own individual DNA to offer colleges. This puts them in more control than they might originally have thought.

Scheduling interviews with not only the head of admissions but with faculty and department heads in the area of your student's interests shows **demonstrable interest**. Many department chairs would like to be part of the admissions process and scheduling an interview with them demonstrates a high level of maturity.

While scheduling these interviews the student should be looking for areas of **institutional need** that they may be able to satisfy and increase their value to the school.

*Anita was the single parent of Linda, an above average student with aspirations of becoming a teacher. Right from the start it became apparent that Linda was a highly disciplined student. Her good grades earned her a 3.47 g.p.a., she participated in sports (varsity field hockey), and played the oboe in the school orchestra.*

*To ensure that there was a good "Fit" for Linda, and an annual college budget of only $10,000, were the main reasons Anita desired*

to work with me. *The option of attending a community college for the first two years was discussed with the family but was not their first choice. Because of reported difficulties getting classes and the time to graduation averaging 6.4 years, the local state university was not an option either.*

*Linda was passionate about becoming a teacher and loved the idea of emulating the practices of the best instructors she had as a student by using hands-on instruction. Based upon her interests a liberal arts curriculum (major) was recommended along with the consideration to apply at small to medium sized colleges. She applied to eight (8) schools and before Christmas she had received letters of acceptance from all eight schools.*

*The next step in the process was to visit the top four campuses on Linda's priority list. The main goal was to make sure that the "Fit" was good for Linda and for her to get tagged by the institution. After completing her visits the number three (3) school initially on her list had jumped to number one (1); a small private college in Oregon. She met with the chairperson for the English department who pointed out the school's record of a 95% graduation rate in four (4) years or less and a 90% employment rate upon graduation.*

*The look and feel of the campus was ideal for Linda. After her thorough investigation she stated that it felt comfortable and almost like being at home. Linda also met with the director of the orchestra and the coach for the field hockey team. She thought playing in the orchestra or field hockey might be an option during her years as an upper classman while getting excellent grades was the priority.*

The first of April the Student Aid Reports (SAR) arrived from each school that accepted Linda's application for attendance. Offers of financial aid came in from her third, fourth, and sixth ranked schools in amounts that made the college budget work for mom (Anita). Linda's top school choice, in Oregon, made an offer that was $7,000 over the family budget. Linda was extremely disappointed and wanted to know if there was anything that could be done to improve the top school offer.

I suggested that she contact the Orchestra Director and the Field Hockey Coach to see if she could participate in their venue as a Freshman. During her conversation with the Orchestra Director she found out that due to graduation, there were two (2) open chairs for Oboe players. Linda quickly drafted a letter to the Orchestra Director stating her desire to play immediately upon admission and provided a list of her awards and accomplishments with the Oboe. A copy of the letter was also sent to the Director of Admissions requesting a reconsideration of the original SAR (offer) due to the added value Linda was going to bring to the college by playing in the orchestra.

Within a week a new SAR had been sent to Linda from the school in Oregon. The new SAR added a "Free Money" award of $12,500 above the initial offer! Now Linda could attend her dream school for $5,000 **under** the family college budget. Both Linda and Anita were beyond happy, almost in disbelief. Everything worked out well within the parameters of their financial plan for college.

Because Linda was able to uncover an **institutional need** that she could fill, more financial aid was provided by the school. This *meant that she would not have to take out any student loans in order to pursue her choice of career while attending her dream school.*

Colleges don't like to be rejected so getting to know and understand your student gives them a higher degree of confidence that their offer for admission will be accepted. Getting to know the atmosphere, the DNA, the departments, faculty, and other students of each college gives your student a clearer idea of whether or not it's a good fit for them. It also shows the college the demonstrable interest that they are looking for from valued students.

While schools frequently measure the demonstrable interest of each student it is imperative that the student and family fulfill their own due diligence to ensure success. Have your student prepare a list of questions for their interview process. It's more important that your son or daughter interview the school than it is for the school to interview them.

Essential questions about the qualities needed for success in the department, undergraduate research opportunities, leadership positions, and most importantly job placement statistics within the first year of graduation are the types of questions that will get the college's attention and position your student for higher consideration.

During the interview your student should discuss current activities (the MAs) and high school activities. The interview process itself demonstrates maturity and students should be prepared to assert themselves and ask the department chair or other faculty member outright if they think that they would be a good fit at the school.

When the answer is yes about fitting in ask that the individual support your submission and request that they call your contact in admissions and recommend your acceptance. Again this is a mature move that can pay huge dividends. **If this is the school of your dreams don't be afraid to ask for their support of your efforts.**

Why is it important to bring up activities and interests during the interview? Remember the tuba player example earlier? If your student mentions their tuba playing in the marching band and the admission director knows that the school needs tuba players your student just earned another tag on their application. This increased the value of the student to the school.

**Being unique and setting them self apart at selective and competitive schools will enhance your student's chances for admission.**

The more information your student has about what the college is looking for helps them determine whether it is the right school for them and if they will fit in. Keep in mind that the choice of their college is not a four-year decision…it's a 40 year decision.

A campus visit is a great way to learn more about a college and it's vitally important to attend during a typical day when classes are in session and not on the official campus visit day when the red carpet is rolled out. Your student will want to experience an average day on which they can attend a class, visit the Student Union and Library, eat cafeteria food, and speak with as many current students on campus as possible.

Visits should begin early in your student's senior year of high school in order to help them narrow down their final decision. At this point the applications have already been submitted and you are conducting your due diligence.

**Guideline for a Successful Campus Visit:**

- Visit only when classes are in session. Ideally visit Tuesday through Thursday when the majority of students are attending classes.

- Walk the campus. Inspect the dorms, Library, and Student Union. Arrange to eat at the cafeteria in order to make sure that they meet your culinary expectations.

- Talk with as many students as possible and ask what they value about the school and what they struggle with.

- Prior to your visit spend some time monitoring Social Media sites that highlight day-to-day life on campus and pay attention to recurring compliments or complaints.

- Audit one class during your visit. Make these arrangements with the department head of the area you want to major in. It's best to contact them directly rather than go through the admissions office as they will most likely urge you to attend a formal campus visit day.

In addition to talking to admissions, faculty and students, drive the neighborhoods and get a feel for the area. Consider if environmental differences such as climate or urban versus small town would be distractions or a welcomed opportunity.

Parents play an important role in the visitation process as well. As your student gains a clear understanding of the school's expectation it often helps reduce their anxiety as well as yours as it relates to whether the school is the right fit. While you may consider visitations as an extra expense by doing your due diligence you can prevent an even costlier event if your student ends up at the wrong school.

## Interview Strategy

Whenever possible schedule meetings with not only the head of the admissions department but with the Chairperson of the department you want to major in as well. During the meeting your aim is to strategically redirect the interviewing process from them interviewing you to you doing the interviewing. This will allow you to demonstrate qualities that will set you apart from the other interviewees.

As the interview begins you will probably be asked why you want to attend their school. This is a great opportunity to redirect the process by answering something to this order:

- That's a great question and I'm glad you asked. I've done quite a bit of research and investigation into colleges that would be the best fit for me as well as me being the best fit for the college and honestly your college is at the top of my list.

- I've researched the (major) Department and I know how challenging this curriculum is going to be so to answer your question-that is exactly why I am here-to find out why I DO want to attend.

- You could have easily been the head if the (major) Department at any number of colleges. Why did you pick this college? (Give them time to answer and take notes)

- What qualities would a student need to possess in order to be successful here?

- Where do you see most of the incoming freshmen make mistakes?

- One area that is highly interesting to me is _____. How does your department and current curriculum prepare me for a successful career in that field?

- If you were going to recommend a student for admission here what would that student have to demonstrate in order to gain your support?

- As an incoming freshman what direction or advice would you give me regarding the one thing I should always apply, or always do during my undergraduate studies?

- Having researched and investigated both the college and the tough curriculum requirements for a major in this department if I have difficulties in transitioning from high school into college, how can I gain additional assistance to make sure my studies don't fall behind?

- Are there any other colleges that you think would be a good idea for me to consider?
- What specifically do I need to do in order to get a head start before attending college next fall?
- From our conversation I know that you believe the choice a student makes regarding the college they attend is very important and should not be taken lightly. Thank you so much for the time you have taken with me today. I certainly appreciate it. I look forward to seeing you again in the fall.

As mentioned earlier, if you feel the interview went well don't be afraid to ask for an endorsement and an acceptance recommendation. Make sure you have the name of your contact in admissions available.

For more information on setting yourself apart, go to:
www.collegewithoutstudentloans.com/setapart.html

# Chapter 8

# EXECUTION

"Start with the end in mind."
**— Stephen R. Covey**

Now that you've gotten an inside look at how desirable schools will compete for your student it's time to use that information to your student's best advantage.

*David, the only child of Bruce and Joanne, attends a highly regarded private high school. As an excellent student David had many career options that he could focus his efforts upon. During his sophomore year of high school he told his parents that he wanted to become a doctor. Bruce had two immediate reactions; one of pride for his son, and one of panic due to the expense of medical school and the fact that the amount they had saved was for college only and did not include enough for a higher level of education.*

*Bruce and Joanne asked me to help them develop an effective plan that met David's goal of being a doctor and their objective of supporting their son without going broke in the process. My expertise was sought because David's private high school was very good at getting their students accepted to elite undergraduate schools but did not provide any financial guidance to the families whatsoever. Bruce was very successful in his profession and Joanne did not work out side of the home. Their income level would be considered upper middle class so there would definitely be no "Need" based aid for this family.*

*The first thing we did was agree to ensure that the "Fit" of working in the medical field was the correct focus. David participated in an internship program at the local hospital which became the true test of his desire to be in the medical field. During the summer and into his junior year of high school he worked in the hospital in various capacities and really enjoyed himself. This further committed him to the direction of medicine.*

***The next step was to decide which medical school David wanted to graduate from.*** *My preferred method when working with students who have aspirations for advanced degrees (i.e., master, PhD, MD) is to establish the end destination and then work backwards to develop a plan. After a thorough investigation of possible schools David wanted to graduate from either an elite*

*or very selective medical school. He additionally believed that he wanted to attend an elite school (Stanford) for his undergraduate degree based on the advice he received from his high school counselor. It was clear to me that working with the college budget set by Bruce that an elite undergraduate program would have two negative effects; first David would be competing against the highest caliber of undergraduates for grades, and second the expense would eat up most if not all of the money established for his education necessitating the consideration of using student loans. I suggested the option of attending a selective or competitive level undergrad program and then move up to the elite medical school rather than initially attending an elite undergrad and med school program.*

*Reviewing all of the options David decided to apply to five (5) selective universities and two (2) elite schools for his undergraduate studies. He was accepted at all seven (7) schools. When the Student Aid Reports (SAR) arrived it was clear that the larger "Merit" aid awards came from the selective schools by almost $10,000 per year. As it turned out three (3) of the selective schools offered a full tuition and books award which meant Bruce and Joanne only had the cost of living expenses to cover. This left a substantial amount of money in the bank to pay for medical school.*

*David is excelling academically at the selective school he chose to attend and now has the choice of attending three (3) different elite medical schools. By executing an effective plan this family was able to allow their son to attend the best schools, eliminate the need for student loans, and fulfill their dreams.*

While developing the plan is important the execution is essential. Applying early is a form of demonstrable interest and typically the applicant gets a more favorable review from admissions than someone who just squeaks in at the deadline. In essence the longer your student waits the fiercer the competition for the remaining seats becomes.

Applying early is a great strategy and can be used for leverage between schools with attractive offers. Here's where knowing the difference can help your student find the best fit and the best financial aid package.

With an admissions process that is both objective and subjective and despite doing "everything right" less than 8% of applicants are accepted at many highly recognized schools.

While that may seem to be a discouraging statistic the odds increase dramatically as the student ferrets out the ideal fits from the good fits as we discussed in the Selection chapter. Working ahead of schedule allows your student time to fine tune the application and get valuable **unhurried** input from counselors and professionals. Requesting high school transcripts, letters of recommendation, and ACT/SAT scores all take time to coordinate.

The student then needs to complete the common application questions and write their essays. We both know that an essay written at 11:30 PM the night before the application needs to be postmarked is probably not going to impress the reviewers.

While I encourage feedback from numerous sources on the application and essay **it is imperative that your student do the work**. They may incorporate suggestions and ideas but if the essay or application seems too polished it may be rejected.

The application process may be considered a part time job throughout the summer between the junior year and the first semester of your student's senior year.

It is not your job as a parent to gather applications, develop essay ideas, or schedule your student's visits. Allowing them to take the lead, make arrangements, and feel in control of the process is the best way to equip your student for their college experience. You however know your student better than anyone else and can provide valuable support and input on their ideas, application questions, and criteria for choosing essay topics. It's a delicate balance but hasn't every other aspect of parenting been that way so far as well?

Exceeding deadlines can work wonders in getting a school's attention and as a side benefit it takes the last minute pressure off of you and your student. The sooner you nudge your student in that direction the better.

Execution Timeline:

* **May** - Decision for Attendance - Each Student Commits to Their School of Choice
* **April** - Student Aid Reports (SAR) arrive, review for accuracy, submit reconsideration letters
* **March** - Final Acceptance Letters Arrive, Last School Visits
* **February** - Visit Schools that have Accepted Your Application
* **January** - Submit the FAFSA and CSS Profiles, Set Up School Visits
* **December** - Acceptance Letters Begin Arriving
* **November** - Re-take SAT/ACT, if needed
* **October** - Submit Applications with Letters of Recommendation
* **September** - SAT/ACT test, Complete College Applications
* **August** - Select Colleges for Application, Finalize Essays

Junior: **SAT/ACT Prep, Select Major, Review Colleges**

Sophomore: **PSAT Test, Career Direction, Funding Plan**

Freshman: **Likes & Dislikes, College Funding Plan**

## Execution Timeline:

- Freshman & Sophomore Year – Focus on SAT/ACT preparation and fine tune career interests.

- Junior Year – Continue preparation for SAT/ACT. Participate in volunteer and extracurricular activities that will strengthen their overall profile.
  - ◊ January through May – Refine list of schools to apply to and ensure a good fit.
  - ◊ Summer – Obtain requirements plus all admission applications and begin to complete them and work on the required essays.
- Senior Year – Continue participation in volunteer and extracurricular activities.
  - ◊ September – Fine tune applications and request letters of recommendation from teachers, counselors, coaches, and mentors.
  - ◊ October – Submit applications and begin applications for financial aid.
  - ◊ November and December – Contact potential schools and arrange for personal visits and interviews.
  - ◊ January – Submit the FAFSA and CSS profile.
  - ◊ February and March – Follow up with potential schools and schedule personal visits with additional schools if desired.
  - ◊ March – Acceptance/Waiting List/Denial letters will start arriving.
  - ◊ April – Student Aid Report (SAR) awards and offers of acceptance from individual schools will begin to

arrive. Review each SAR for accuracy and notify the school's department of admission prior to end of month.

◊   May – Commit to the school of choice.

## Go Get It

Since the beginning of this book I've worked to dispel the myths surrounding elite schools, financial aid, and the selection process utilized by institutions of higher learning. By now you have a clear picture of the opportunities available to you and your student through planning, preparation, and positioning.

As of this writing, there is a backlash beginning to rumble though the media on the over-inflated cost of college, rising student loan debt, and the value of mass education. My goal is to provide you with the realization that college without student loans is not only possible but an achievable reality for every family.

Student and parent college debt is most likely the next economic bubble to burst which will have a devastating impact on the quality of life families will be able to enjoy. If I have helped just one family eliminate a student loan then I have accomplished my mission.

Through the S-A-F-E process you and your student will exercise due diligence, carefully consider what makes a good fit, apply with confidence, and select from attractive offers made by each student's ideal school. Every student that applies the methods and principle of this process will have a better educational result and a more positive direction in life. **I guarantee it!**

For more information about execution, go to:

www.collegewithoutstudentloans.com/execution.html

# About The Author

I WAS BORN IN southern California in the middle of the baby boom of the 1950s and was raised in a household like most middle class families. My parents were honest, hardworking, and living the American Dream.

Education was the key to getting ahead in life and this coupled with a strong work ethic was my formula for success. I worked hard from the day I turned 16 years old and achieved good grades in school so I could get into college. Taking my parent's advice I went to a local college and then to Europe for nearly two school years. Studying in Sweden exposed me to the ways and customs of others which turned out to be one of the best decisions I've ever made.

This diverse education fostered my belief that there are many different ways to accomplish a goal. Having earned a Business Management Degree from a highly ranked state college was merely a springboard for my career.

Starting in the medical device industry I found sales stimulating because everything I did was focused on solving a problem that my client was experiencing. Problems are just puzzles that need a solution. I became very good at providing solutions which led to me being promoted up the corporate ladder.

The more puzzles I solved the more success came my way, something that has been a constant in my life. An early mentor, Zig Ziglar had a motto: "You will get everything you want out of life IF you help enough people get what they want." This has been so true for me.

Accepting the request of my mother to ensure that all of the children in our family graduate from college and not be burdened with financial obligations was the start of my journey which has resulted in the creation of this book.